READY, SET, GROW: ANIMALS

A TURTLE GROWS

by Rex Ruby

Consultant: Beth Gambro,
Reading Specialist, Yorkville, Illinois

Minneapolis, Minnesota

Teaching Tips

Before Reading

- Look at the cover of the book. Discuss the picture and the title.
- Ask readers to brainstorm a list of what they already know about turtles. What can they expect to see in the book?
- Go on a picture walk, looking through the pictures to discuss vocabulary and make predictions about the text.

During Reading

- Read for purpose. Encourage readers to think about how a turtle grows as they are reading.
- Ask readers to look for the details of the book. What are they learning about different stages of the growing process?
- If readers encounter an unknown word, ask them to look at the sounds in the word. Then, ask them to look at the rest of the page. Are there any clues to help them understand?

After Reading

- Encourage readers to pick a buddy and reread the book together.
- Ask readers to name two things that happen as a turtle grows. Find the pages that tell about these things.
- Ask readers to write or draw something they learned about turtles.

Credits

Cover and title page, © sdominick/iStock; 3, © Rosa Jay/Shutterstock; 5, © Danita Delimont/Shutterstock; 6–7, © Maui Topical Images/Shutterstock; 9, © Elizabeth Caron/Shutterstock; 11, © Akashi, H/ Kubota, M./Yamamoto, H./www.nature.com/articles/s41598-022-15515-w; 13, © Wild Wonders of Europe/Zankl/Nature Picture Library; 15, © Martin Pelanek/Shutterstock; 17, © Mark Lotterhand/Adobe Stock; 19, © ChristinaPrinn/Getty Images; 20-21, © Tui De Roy/Minden Pictures; 22TR, © Zoonar GmbH/Alamy Stock Photo; 22ML, © Issouf Sanogo/Getty Images; 22BR, © Tom Helinski/Adobe Stock; 23TL, © Denisyuk Alexsander/Adobe Stock; 23TM, © Akashi, H/ Kubota, M./Yamamoto, H./www.nature.com/articles/s41598-022-15515-w; 23TR, © Elizabeth Caron/Shutterstock; 23BL, © Jason Edwards/Getty Images; 23BM, © Jan Corradini/Adobe Stock; 23BR, © Don Serhio/Adobe Stock

See BearportPublishing.com for our statement on Generative AI Usage.

Library of Congress Cataloging-in-Publication Data is available at www.loc.gov or upon request from the publisher.

ISBN: 979-8-89232-997-2 (hardcover)
ISBN: 979-8-89577-428-1 (paperback)
ISBN: 979-8-89577-114-3 (ebook)

Copyright © 2026 Bearport Publishing Company. All rights reserved. No part of this publication may be reproduced in whole or in part, stored in any retrieval system, or transmitted in any form or by any means, electronic, mechanical, photocopying, recording, or otherwise, without written permission from the publisher. Bearport Publishing is a division of FlutterBee Education Group.

For more information, write to Bearport Publishing, 3500 American Blvd W, Suite 150, Bloomington, MN 55431.

Contents

Shelled Swimmer 4

Turtle Facts 22

Glossary 23

Index 24

Read More 24

Learn More Online 24

About the Author 24

Shelled Swimmer

A turtle crawls on a log by the water.

It has a hard shell and sharp claws.

How did it get this way?

There are many kinds of turtles.

Most of them **mate** in the spring.

After that, eggs form inside the **female** turtle's body.

The female turtle climbs onto land to dig a hole.

She lays her eggs in the hole.

Then, she covers them with sand and dirt.

9

Inside each egg is an **embryo**.

This little baby grows bigger each day.

It forms legs and a tail.

The embryo grows a shell, too.

Say embryo like
EM-bree-*oh*

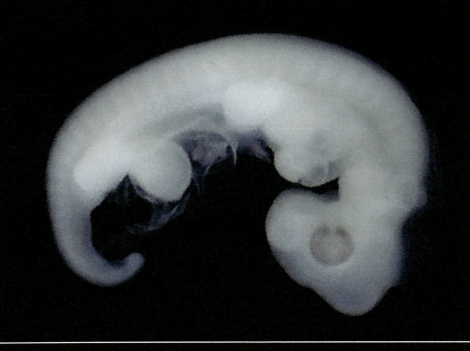

After about 10 weeks, the baby **hatches**.

The turtle opens the egg with its **beak**.

It can take days for the baby to break free.

This little turtle is called a hatchling.

It digs its way out of the dirt and sand.

Then, it quickly hides in water or under leaves.

Soon, the hatchling looks for food.

It eats plants.

It may also feed on small animals.

The baby turtle grows bigger.

17

The young turtle's shell needs to grow, too.

How?

The shell has plates called **scutes**.

The old scutes fall off.

Then, larger ones grow in.

The turtle gets much larger.

After many years, the turtle becomes an adult.

Then, it can make its own eggs!

Turtle Facts

There are more than 350 kinds of turtles.

Some turtles live to be more than 100 years old!

Leatherback turtles are the biggest turtles. They can be longer than a mattress!

Glossary

beak the hard, pointed part of a turtle's mouth

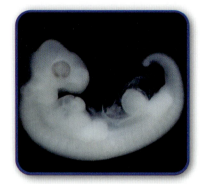

embryo an animal in the first stage of growth

female a turtle that can lay eggs

hatches breaks out of an egg

mate to come together to have young

scutes horny plates or large scales

Index

beak 12
claws 4
eggs 6, 8, 10, 12, 20
embryo 10
food 16
scutes 18–19
shell 4, 10, 18

Read More

Lynch, Seth. *Turtles Close Up (Animals Close Up).* New York: Gareth Stevens Publishing, 2023.

Neuenfeldt, Elizabeth. *Baby Turtles (Too Cute!).* Minneapolis: Bellwether Media, 2024.

Learn More Online

1. Go to **FactSurfer.com** or scan the QR code below.
2. Enter "**Turtles Grow**" into the search box.
3. Click on the cover of this book to see a list of websites.

About the Author

Rex Ruby lives in Minnesota with his family. He enjoys seeing turtles by the pond.